LIKE ANYBODY ELSE, OR MAYBE MORESO, AL GORE IS A COMPLEX FIGURE FULL OF CONTRADICTIONS.

A SON OF PRIVILEGE. AN ADVOCATE FOR THE COMMON MAN.

A SCION OF A POWERFUL POLITICAL FAMILY GROOMED FOR THE PRESIDENCY. A CRUSADER FOR PUBLIC SERVICE.

EARLY CAMPAIGNS FUNDED BY OIL PROFITS. A TIRELESS ACTIVIST AGAINST THE RAVAGES OF A FOSSIL-FUEL ADDICTED WORLD.

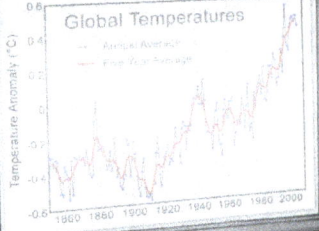

A CAGEY POLITICIAN. A MAN CAPABLE OF SOPHOMORIC EXAGGERATIONS AND GENERALIZATIONS.

WOODEN AND SERIOUS, YET SELF-DEPRECATING AND PLAYFUL.

ENLISTED AND SERVED IN THE VIETNAM WAR DESPITE HIS OPPOSITION TO THE WAR AND CHOSE NOT TO USE HIS CONNECTIONS TO AVOID SERVING IN-COUNTRY.

A MAN HARDENED BY THE CUTTHROAT WORLD OF WASHINGTON DC AND A GENTLEMAN FARMER FROM THE PASTORAL CALM OF CARTHAGE, TENNESSEE.

NOW, EVERY STORY HAS A BEGINNING.

AND TO UNDERSTAND AL GORE, YOU ALSO HAVE TO LOOK AT THE POST-WAR WORLD HE WAS BORN INTO.

GORE'S FATHER GREW UP IN POSSUM HOLLOW TN, A HARD-SCRABBLE FARM TOWN THAT SOUNDED AS IF IT CAME STRAIGHT OUT OF LI'L ABNER.

THE ELDER GORE PUT HIMSELF THROUGH SCHOOL WORKING VARIOUS TEACHING JOBS.

THEN CAME THE CLARION CALL OF POLITICS THAT DREW HIM TO WASHINGTON WHERE HE'D SERVE IN CONGRESS FOR 32 YEARS.

ODDLY ENOUGH, GORE'S FATHER WAS NOT THE FIRST GORE TO HOLD POLITICAL OFFICE.

GORE'S GREAT-GREAT-GREAT GRANDFATHER JOHN GORE FOUGHT IN THE REVOLUTIONARY WAR AND LATER SERVED IN THE TENNESSEE GENERAL ASSEMBLY.

GORE'S MOTHER PAULINE WAS NOT YOUR AVERAGE POLITICAL WIFE.

UNLIKE MANY POLITICAL WIVES OF THE TIME, SHE PLAYED AN ACTIVE ROLE IN HER HUSBAND'S CAMPAIGNS AND WAS HIS CLOSEST ADVISOR.

A SKILLED LAWYER IN HER OWN RIGHT, SHE WAS ONE OF THE FIRST FEMALES TO GRADUATE FROM VANDERBILT UNIVERSITY WITH A LAW DEGREE.

HOWEVER, POLITICS IN THE 1930S WAS STILL A MAN'S WORLD. SHE DISCOVERED THAT HER CONSIDERABLE SMARTS AND DETERMINATION COULD TAKE HER SO FAR.

SHE CHANNELED HER DRIVE IN SHAPING HER HUSBAND'S CAREER AND LATER ON, HER SON'S.

I TRAINED THEM BOTH. AND I DID A BETTER JOB ON MY SON.

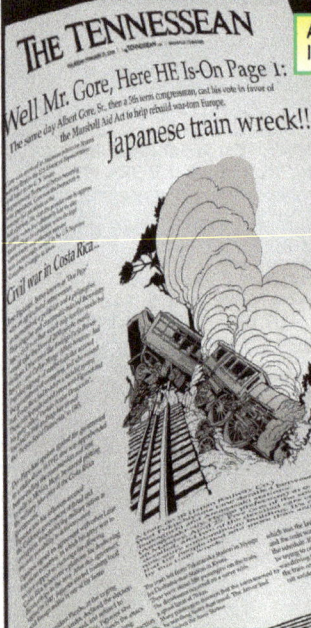

AL GORE WAS BORN INTO POLITICS.

MARCH 31, 1948 IN WASHINGTON DC.

THE SAME DAY ALBERT GORE, SR., THEN A 5TH TERM CONGRESSMAN, CAST HIS VOTE IN FAVOR OF THE MARSHALL AID ACT TO HELP REBUILD WAR-TORN EUROPE.

AL GORE WAS BORN INTO A WORLD OF PRIVILEGE.

QUESTIONS HAVE ALWAYS DOGGED THE GORES AS TO THE SOURCE OF THE FAMILY'S WEALTH.

BUT WITH POWER ALWAYS COMES THE WHISPERINGS OF DOUBT.

SOME POINT TO DECLASSIFIED FBI FILES, THAT SENIOR WAS "IN THE POCKET" OF A KNOWN SOVIET SYMPATHIZER, ALLEGED RUSSIAN SPY AND EXTREMELY WEALTHY INDUSTRIALIST ARMAND HAMMER.

RECORDS SHOW THAT MOST OF THE GORE'S MEANS CAME FROM THEIR FAMILY FARMS AND WISE INVESTING.

THIS PUT HIM IN THE CROSS-HAIRS OF POWERFUL ENEMIES LIKE J. EDGAR HOOVER.

THE SENATOR HARBORS A STRONG PERSONAL ANIMOSITY TOWARDS THE BUREAU.

CLYDE, HE IS NO FRIEND OF THE FBI.

CLASSIFIED

HISTORY SHOWS THAT WASHINGTON IS A WORLD OF SECRETS.

DESPITE THE WEALTH, OR MAYBE BECAUSE OF IT, AL'S EARLY CHILDHOOD SEEMED A LONELY ONE

LIVING IN THE SWANK FAIRFAX HOTEL ALONG EMBASSY ROW, HE GREW UP IN THE AMONGST WASHINGTON'S ELITE AND BELLHOPS.

FOR THE MOST PART IT WAS A VERY STOIC AND STAID ENVIRONMENT.

THAT DIDN'T MEAN "LITTLE AL" DIDN'T HAVE HIS MOMENTS.

DRIVING OLD CRANKY SEN. MCLELLAN CRAZY BY BOUNCING A BASKETBALL UP AND DOWN THE HALLS.

OR DROP WATER BALLOONS ON UNSUSPECTING LIMOUSINES FROM THE ROOF.

I AM CERTAINLY GLAD TO MEET YOUR ACQUAINTANCE, SIR.

YET FROM ALL OBSERVERS YOUNG ALBERT WAS A PRODUCT OF HIS ENVIRONMENT.

HE WAS A PERFECT LITTLE GENTLEMAN. COURTEOUS. EARNEST. DISCIPLINED.

AND WOULD IT SURPRISE YOU, HE WAS AN INCORRIGIBLE TATTLE TALE.

I'M TELLING DAD!

LITTLE AL WAS A PRODUCT OF HIS '50S RIGID, STRUCTURED SURROUNDINGS.

A FRIEND ONCE SAID THAT AL WAS VERY SELF-CONSCIOUSNESS OF ALWAYS HAVING TO BE "ON."

AND HE THRIVED DESPITE THE PRESSURES OF BEING "THE SENATOR'S SON."

IF WE'RE LUCKY, A FEW PEOPLE IN OUR LIVES KEENLY SHAPE OUR ATTITUDES, OUR THOUGHTS AND EVEN OUR ACTIONS.

PAULINE GORE, AL'S MOTHER TOPS THE LIST.

ANOTHER WAS AL'S HEADMASTER AT HIS PRIVATE SCHOOL, CANON CHARLES MARTIN

ALBERT, YOU MUST CHOOSE THE *HARD RIGHT* OVER THE EASY WRONG.

THIS SIMPLE MANTRA CARRIED AL THROUGH HIS YEARS AT THE ELITE ST. ALBANS SCHOOL, HARVARD AND INTO HIS LIFE AS A PUBLIC SERVANT.

HE MADE HIMSELF THE SON THAT HIS PARENTS WANTED AND THE VERY MODEL OF A ST. ALBANS BOY.

HE WAS GOOD AT MOST THINGS, BUT HE WAS NEVER THE BEST.

HE WAS A WELL-TRAINED, DUTIFUL SON

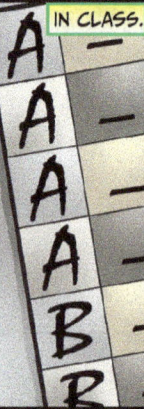

IN CLASS.

IN SPORTS.

IN ART.

OR SCHOOL POLITICS.

GORE FOR SENIOR PREFECT

CLASSMATES RECOGNIZED AL'S NEAR-MANIC DRIVE TO BE PERFECT. ONE TEACHER CALLED HIM "A WOODEN APOLLO."

Ana Marshain

Al Gore

BUT IF HE WAS A STRAIGHT ARROW; THE EMBODIMENT OF OVERACHIEVEMENT AND THE GUY MOST LIKELY YOU WANTED TO HANG FROM THE FLAGPOLE BY HIS UNDERPANTS BECAUSE HE REMINDED THE TEACHER ABOUT THE HOMEWORK...

WHEN HE WENT "HOME" TO THE FARMS IN CARTHAGE HE BECAME A DIFFERENT PERSON.

RELAXED. FUN-LOVING. DARING. IMPETUOUS. EVEN A BIT RECKLESS.

IT'S ONE OF THE REASONS HE THINKS HIMSELF A SOUTHERNER AS OPPOSED TO THAT STIFF-UPPER-LIP RESIDENT OF THE FAIRFAX HOTEL IN DC.

IT'S MORE IN LINE WITH WHAT I THINK HE ASPIRES TO BE.

THE TENNESSEE LIFE TOOK MUCH OF THE STIFFNESS OUT OF GORE.

SUMMERS AND HOLIDAYS, AL TRAVELED TO THE FAMILY FARM IN CARTHAGE; ABOUT 40 MILES EAST OF NASHVILLE.

"EVEN THOUGH I SPENT MORE TIME EACH YEAR IN WASHINGTON, TENNESSEE WAS HOME."

HIS REAL CHILDHOOD WAS IN TENNESSEE;

HERE HE WATER SKIED, HUNG WITH FRIENDS, SNUCK HIS FIRST KISS AND PERFORMED THOSE CRAZY STUNTS PARENTS WOULD CRINGE OVER.

A GIRLFRIEND REFLECTED WHEN HE RETURNED TO TENNESSEE HE "WALKED LIKE A CITY BOY." IT TOOK "ABOUT 2 WEEKS" TO GET COMFORTABLE.

BUT CARTHAGE WAS NOT ALL ABOUT FUN AND RELAXATION. THE ELDER GORE EXPECTED AL TO WORK.

AND HE DID WORK HARD. SO HARD THAT THE HIRED HELP FELT SORRY FOR HIM, AND THOUGHT HIS FATHER SHOULD EASE UP.

HE BALED HAY, CUT TOBACCO AND CLEANED OUT HOG PARLORS ALONG WITH THE HIRED HELP.

HIS FATHER SEEMED TO ENJOY IN ASSIGNING AL SOME OF THE MOST BACKBREAKING TASKS, LIKE CLEARING 20 HILLY ACRES WITH A HAND AX.

BUT IT WAS BACK IN DC WHERE AL WOULD MEET THE LOVE OF HIS LIFE.

AND SHE STARTED OUT AS SOMEONE ELSE'S PROM DATE.

MARY ELIZABETH AITCHESON, NICKNAMED TIPPER, DATED MANY BOYS AT ST. ALBANS

BUT ONCE AL HAD GOT HER PHONE NUMBER, A ROMANCE AND RELATIONSHIP THAT HAS LASTED NEARLY FORTY FIVE YEARS BEGAN.

EVERYDAY THAT SUMMER HE RODE HIS MOTORCYCLE FROM WORK TO THE ATCHISON HOME FOR LUNCH.

BOLOGNA AND CHEESE AGAIN?

CAN'T YOU MAKE ANYTHING ELSE.

NO.

IT WAS LOVE AT FIRST SLICE.

IN THE FALL GORE ENROLLED AT HARVARD.

IT WAS THE ONLY SCHOOL HE APPLIED TO.

IT WASN'T UNTIL THE POLITICAL AND SOCIAL TURMOIL OF 1968 THAT GORE FINALLY TOOK AN INTEREST IN POLITICS.

HE CHANGED HIS MAJOR FROM ENGLISH TO GOVERNMENT.

YES, YES, HE ALSO ROOMED WITH FUTURE ACADEMY AWARD WINNER TOMMY LEE JONES. HAPPY?

WHILE MANY AROUND HIM WERE PROTESTING, AL NEVER ACTIVELY PARTICIPATED.

HE KNEW CHANGE AND SOCIAL PROGRESS HAD TO COME FROM THE INSIDE; NOT FROM SIT-INS.

WITHIN MONTHS OF GRADUATION, GORE ENLISTED IN THE ARMY.

IT WAS 1969. THE VIETNAM WAR WAS RAGING.

MANY CAST A CYNICAL EYE ON GORE'S MILITARY SERVICE.

HE COULD'VE PULLED STRINGS, RECEIVED DEFERMENTS OR LANDED A CUSHY STATESIDE POSTING.

AGAIN AL TOOK THE "HARD RIGHT" OVER THE EASY WRONG.

GORE ENLISTED FOR TWO REASONS: AVOIDING THE WAR MIGHT IMPACT HIS FATHER'S VULNERABLE SENATE SEAT IN 1970.

AND IF HE DIDN'T GO, SOMEONE WITH FEWER ADVANTAGES WOULD.

GORE'S CRITICS DON'T FAULT HIM FOR ENLISTING. IT WAS REVEALED THE NIXON ADMINISTRATION DELAYED HIS DEPLOYMENT OVERSEAS IN FEAR OF THE SYMPATHY EFFECT IT MIGHT HAVE ON SENIOR'S SENATE CAMPAIGN.

NOR DO HIS CRITICS ADMONISH HIM FOR SERVING AS A JOURNALIST STATIONED WITH THE 20TH ENGINEER BRIGADE. WELL SOME DO.

CRITICS LAMBAST GORE FOR HIS ALLEGED EMBELLISHMENTS.

AFTER SEVERAL HISTORY REVISIONS, GORE SAYS THIS ABOUT HIS SERVICE:

SPECIFICALLY REGARDING HIS ROLE IN COMBAT.

I DON'T PRETEND MY MILITARY SERVICE MATCHES IN ANY WAY WHAT OTHERS HAVE BEEN THROUGH.

I DIDN'T DO THE MOST, OR RUN THE GREATEST DANGER. BUT I WAS PROUD TO WEAR MY COUNTRY'S UNIFORM.

HE DESERVES CREDIT FOR HONORABLY SERVING HIS COUNTRY.

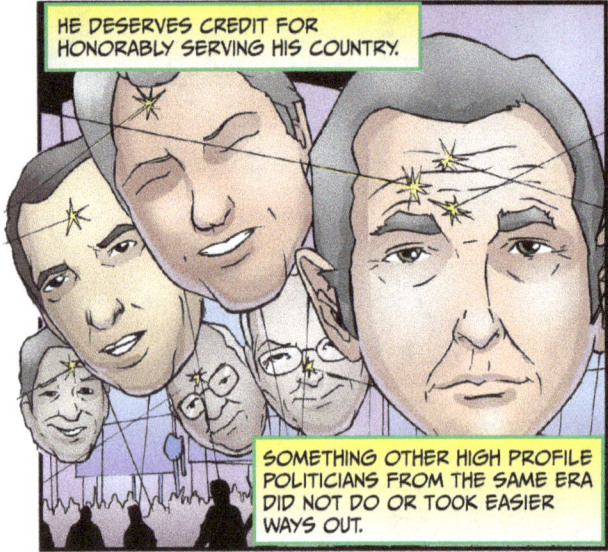

GORE SERVED A TOTAL OF 5 MONTHS IN-COUNTRY IN 1971.

SOMETHING OTHER HIGH PROFILE POLITICIANS FROM THE SAME ERA DID NOT DO OR TOOK EASIER WAYS OUT.

QUICK REWIND...PRIOR TO SHIPPING OUT AL MARRIED TIPPER ON MARCH 19, 1970 IN THE NATIONAL CATHEDRAL IN WASHINGTON DC.

HIS OLD ST ALBANS HEADMASTER CANON CHARLES MARTIN OFFICIATED THE CEREMONY.

AND THE ORGANIST PLAYED THE BEATLES! "ALL YOU NEED IS LOVE."

GORE SAYS HE RETURNED FROM VIETNAM FEELING DISCOURAGED.

DEEP OPPOSITION OF THE WAR COMBINED WITH HIS FATHER'S 1970 SENATORIAL DEFEAT ADDED TO THOSE FEELINGS. AFTER A BRIEF FLIRTATION WITH DIVINITY SCHOOL GORE EMBARKED ON A NEW CAREER. REPORTER FOR THE TENNESSEAN.

GORE ENJOYED MODEST SUCCESS, BUT FINALLY MADE HIS MARK ON THE NASHVILLE METRO BEAT.

THE TENNESSEAN

HIS HIGHLIGHT WAS AN INVESTIGATIVE PIECE ON A CORRUPT COUNCILMAN THAT LED TO AN ARREST.

THE NEWSPAPER REKINDLED INTEREST IN PUBLIC SERVICE. GORE TOOK A LEAVE OF ABSENCE TO ATTEND LAW SCHOOL.

AND *THAT* LED TO ONE PLACE.

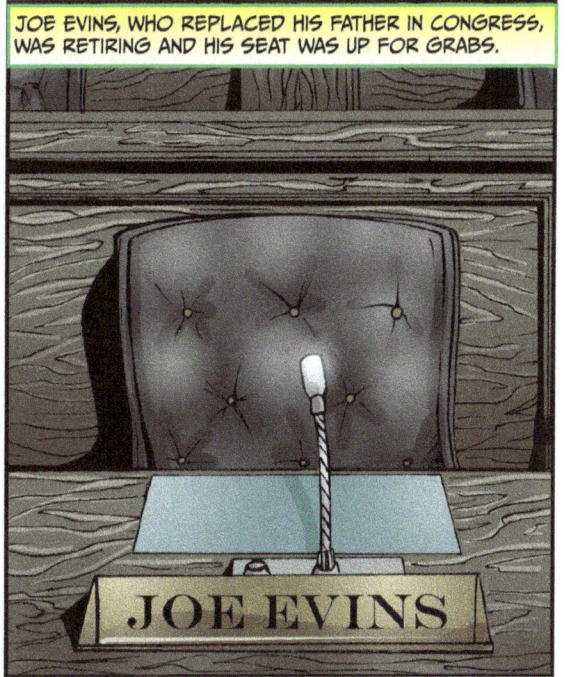

JOE EVINS, WHO REPLACED HIS FATHER IN CONGRESS, WAS RETIRING AND HIS SEAT WAS UP FOR GRABS.

JOE EVINS

I SUPPORTED YOUR FATHER, AND I'LL SUPPORT YOU TOO!

HIS MOTHER, JUST AS SHE DID FOR AL'S FATHER, PLAYED A KEY ROLE IN SETTING UP HER SON FOR SUCCESS.

DETERMINED TO BE HIS OWN MAN HE WAS STILL IN THE SHADOW OF HIS PARENTS.

THAT INCLUDED A POWERFUL LEGACY AND SUSPECTED DUBIOUS ASSOCIATIONS.

GORE RECEIVED 32% OF THE VOTE AND WON THE SEAT.

SO AT AGE 28, LITTLE AL WAS NOW REPRESENTATIVE ALBERT A GORE, JR OF THE 4TH DISTRICT OF TENNESSEE.

DURING MY SERVICE IN THE US CONGRESS, I TOOK THE INITIATIVE IN CREATING THE INTERNET.

(3/9/99)

IT'S NOT THAT IT'S A FALSEHOOD.

HE *DID* CHAIR THE COMMITTEE. HE *DID* UNDERSTAND AND SUPPORT THE COMMERCIAL POTENTIAL OF THE EXISTING APPLICATION.

HE EVEN COINED THE TERM INFORMATION SUPERHIGHWAY.

BUT INVENT IT, THAT'S A STRETCH.

ANOTHER EXAMPLE OF GORE'S PENCHANCE FOR EXAGGERATION.

HE HELD THE FIRST CONGRESSIONAL HEARINGS ON CLIMATE CHANGE.

C-SPAN

AND, HE WAS THE FIRST MEMBER OF CONGRESS TO APPEAR ON C-SPAN IN 1979

HE WON RE-ELECTION THREE TIMES BEFORE HE DECIDED TO RUN FOR HIS FATHER'S OLD SENATE SEAT IN 1984.

ENTER SENATOR ALBERT GORE, JR. OF TENNESSEE.

GORE'S SENATE VOTING RECORD SHOWED HE WAS A CENTRIST; BALANCING HIS CONSTITUENCIES' CONSERVATIVE LEANINGS AND HIS OWN MORE IDEALISTIC BELIEFS.

HE DEVELOPED A REPUTATION AS AN INFLEXIBLE PRAGMATIST.

OFTEN TAKING POSITIONS OF MORAL SUPERIORITY.

CONSISTENT WITH HIS "HARD RIGHT" PHILOSOPHY; IT'S A SIMILAR PERSONALITY TRAIT FOR WHICH GEORGE W BUSH IS CRITICIZED.

BUT HE HAD THE INTELLECT TO PROCESS COMPLEX ISSUES LIKE NUCLEAR ARMS CONTROL.

SOME THINK HIS INTEREST IN THE SUBJECT WAS SELF-SERVING. IT WAS A MEATY ISSUE THAT WOULD HELP HIM RISE TO THE NEXT LEVEL

THE PRESIDENCY.

REGARDLESS, GORE'S AMBITION MADE HIM INTO AN EXPERT.

IN 1988, WHEN CONSERVATIVE MOVEMENT USHERED IN BY RONALD REAGAN SEEMED TO BE WANING.

AL GORE
★★★ '88

AL GORE, AT 40, DECIDED TO RUN FOR PRESIDENT.

GORE THOUGHT HE WOULD WIN A LION'S SHARE OF DELEGATES IN THE 12-SOUTHERN STATE PRIMARY NICKNAMED SUPER TUESDAY.

INSTEAD HE SPLIT THE STATES WITH ACTIVIST JESSE JACKSON.

AFTER A POOR SHOWING IN THE NEW YORK PRIMARY, HE BOWED OUT OF THE RACE.

AFTER HIS FAILED PRESIDENTIAL BID, GORE ENDURED SOMETHING NO PARENT SHOULD EXPERIENCE.

HIS SON WAS GRAVELY INJURED IN AN ACCIDENT.

IT'S ENOUGH TO SAY THE MOMENT WAS PRIVATE, INDELIBLE AND TRANSFORMING; AND ONE OF THE REASONS HE CHOSE NOT TO RUN FOR PRESIDENT IN 1992.

THE INTEGRITY OF THE ENVIRONMENT IS NOT ANOTHER ISSUE TO BE USED IN POLITICAL GAMES.

HE FOCUSED ON FAMILY AND REDOUBLED INTEREST IN ENVIRONMENTAL ISSUES.

ONE RESULT WAS THE BEST SELLING BOOK EARTH IN THE BALANCE.

IN 1992 GORE HESITATED TO ACCEPT BILL CLINTON'S OFFER TO BECOME HIS RUNNING MATE.

BEFORE THE ELECTION, THEY HARDLY KNEW ONE ANOTHER.

OTHER THAN THEIR UPBRINGING, THEY SEEMED VERY SIMILAR.

GEORGE BUSH'S URBAN POLICY HAS BEEN A TALE OF 2 CITIES; THE BEST OF TIMES FOR THE VERY WEALTHY; THE WORST OF TIMES FOR EVERYONE ELSE.

BOTH WERE SOUTHERNERS.

BOTH WERE PRODUCTS OF THE BABY BOOM GENERATION.

BOTH WERE DRIVEN.

BOTH WERE POLICY WONKS WHO AGREED ON MOST ISSUES.

BUT THEY WERE QUITE DIFFERENT.

CLINTON SEEMED MORE LIKE A ROCK STAR.

GORE CAME ACROSS AS A WOODEN KNOW-IT-ALL;

CLINTON FELT POLITICS AS A PASSION.

GORE SAW IT AS A CHORE.

HOW CAN YOU TELL AL GORE FROM A ROOM FULL OF SECRET SERVICE AGENTS? GORE IS THE STIFF ONE.

THROUGHOUT THE CAMPAIGN AL WAS TRIED TO SHED HIS SERIOUS, WOODEN IMAGE.

JOHN ADAMS ONCE SAID "MY COUNTRY HAS CONTRIVED FOR ME THE MOST INSIGNIFICANT OFFICE THAT EVER THE INVENTION OF MAN CONTRIVED OR HIS IMAGINATION CONCEIVED."

HE WAS TALKING ABOUT THE VICE PRESIDENCY.

GORE AGREED TO BE VICE PRESIDENT ONLY IF HE WAS GIVEN REAL RESPONSIBILITY

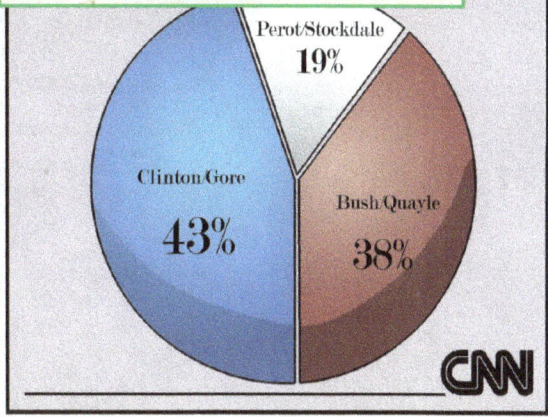

Perot/Stockdale
19%

Clinton Gore
43%

Bush/Quayle
38%

CNN

GORE CHANGED THE VERY MODEL OF THE VICE PRESIDENCY FROM THE GUY WHO GOES TO STATE FUNERALS TO AN EXECUTIVE BRANCH ADVISOR AND POLICY PARTNER.

THOUGH AT TIMES GORE FOUND IT DIFFICULT TO SUCCESSFULLY MOVE HIS AGENDAS.

IN HIS EIGHT YEARS AS VP HE PROMOTED THE ENVIRONMENT AGENDA, ADVISED ON NATIONAL SECURITY, NEGOTIATED TRADE AGREEMENTS AND ROOTED OUT WASTEFUL GOVERNMENT.

NOT ONLY FROM A REPUBLICAN CONTROLLED CONGRESS, BUT WITHIN CLINTON'S INNER CIRCLE TOO.

MEET THE PRESS

HE IS THE PRESIDENT OF THE COUNTRY. HE IS MY FRIEND

IN PUBLIC GORE WAS A DUTIFUL SECOND IN COMMAND.

BEHIND THE SCENES HE WAS DISTURBED BY THE FREQUENT SCANDALS.

AND HOW THEY MIGHT AFFECT HIS OWN POLITICAL FUTURE.

WE COULD SPEND PAGES DECRYING QUESTIONABLE FUNDRAISING, SUSPECT ETHICS AND CHRONIC FOOT IN MOUTH DISEASE...

BUT, HOWEVER YOU SEE TRUTH, THERE'S SOMEONE ELSE JUST AS CERTAIN YOU'RE WRONG.

IF YOU ENTRUST ME WITH THE PRESIDENCY, I WILL MARSHALL ITS AUTHORITY, ITS RESOURCES AND ITS MORAL LEADERSHIP TO FIGHT FOR AMERICA'S FAMILIES.

ON JUNE 16TH 1999, GORE ANNOUNCED HIS 2ND BID FOR THE PRESIDENCY.

THIS TIME HIS RUN WOULD END WITH THE MOST CONTROVERSIAL RESULT IN OVER 100 YEARS.

THE CAMPAIGN FOCUSED ON DOMESTIC ISSUES LIKE THE BUDGET SURPLUS, REFORMS TO SOCIAL SECURITY AND MEDICARE.

BUT MOST NOATABLY GORE'S CAMPAIGN DISTANCED ITSELF FROM BILL CLINTON.

STRATEGISTS WERE WORRIED THAT THE TARNISHED PRESIDENT MIGHT TAINT GORE.

THEN CAME THAT WEIRD, AWKWARD KISS AT THE DEMOCRATIC NATIONAL CONVENTION.

WHAT WAS DEBATED AS A SPONTANEOUS AND ROMANTIC DISPLAY OR A SCRIPTED, PREMEDITATED PHOTO OP TO CHANGE HIS ROBOTIC IMAGE AND FRAME HIM AS A LOVING AND FAITHFUL FAMILY MAN, IT WAS IN ALL PROBABILITY A LITTLE OF BOTH.

IT WAS THE "KISS HEARD 'ROUND THE WORLD" AND IT ONLY LASTED 3 SECONDS.

A DEAD HEAT CAME DOWN TO FLORIDA.

WHOEVER HAD THE MOST VOTES IN A STATE WITH THE CRUCIAL 25 ELECTORAL VOTES WOULD BE PRESIDENT.

BUT NO ONE COULD AGREE ON WHICH VOTES COUNTED, WHICH WERE INELIGIBLE.

NEW WORDS LIKE BUTTERFLY BALLOT, VOTER INTENT AND HANGING CHAD ENTERED THE AMERICAN VOCABULARY.

LAWSUITS, RECOUNTS, POLITICAL SPIN AND WRANGLING, DIRTY TRICKS, AND STRONG ARM TACTICS PUT THE FINAL DECISION IN THE HANDS OF THE 9 JUSTICES OF THE SUPREME COURT.

IN THE END AL GORE GARNERED 50,999,897 VOTES TO GEORGE BUSH'S 50,456,002.

AND GEORGE BUSH BECAME THE 43RD PRESIDENT OF THE UNITED STATES.

SOME POINT TO FRINGE CANDIDATE RALPH NADER'S SIPHONING 2.7% OF THE VOTE AWAY FROM GORE.

OTHERS POINT TO HIS POPULIST CAMPAIGN DID NOT DISTANCE ITSELF FROM THE DISGRACED CLINTON PRESIDENCY.

GORE CONCEDES.

THE STRENGTH OF OUR AMERICAN DEMOCRACY IS SHOWN MOST CLEARLY THROUGH THE DIFFICULTIES IT CAN OVERCOME.

HISTORY BOOKS REMIND US THAT A PEACEFUL TRANSFER OF POWER TOOK PLACE, BUT THE AFTERMATH CREATED AN UGLIER PARTISAN DIVIDE THAT TURNED US ALL INTO RED STATES AND BLUE STATES.

BUT SOONAFTER AL GORE SAW THINGS DIFFERENT...HE SAW US ALL AS GREEN STATES.

THOUGH RUMORS PERSISTED OF ANOTHER PRESIDENTIAL RUN IN 2004 AND 2008,

GORE FOCUSED HIS TIME AND ENERGY IN BEING A PRIMARY FORCE FOR THE BURGEONING GREEN MOVEMENT.

GORE HAD WRITTEN EARTH IN THE BALANCE IN 1992.

AND NOW TRAVELED THE WORLD WARNING AGAINST THE POTENTIAL HAZARDS OF CLIMATE CHANGE.

IF YOU LOOK AT THE 10 HOTTEST YEARS EVER MEASURED, THEY'VE ALL OCCURRED IN THE PAST 14 YEARS.

PROMOTING THE BENEFITS OF RENEWABLE ENERGIES.

PUSHING THE AGENDA FORWARD OF A CARBON-NEUTRAL WORLD.

OUR WORLD FACES A TRUE PLANETARY EMERGENCY

I KNOW THE PHRASE SOUNDS SHRILL, AND I KNOW IT'S A CHALLENGE TO THE MORAL IMAGINATION.

IN 2006 GORE PARTICIPATED IN THE SUCCESSFUL DOCUMENTARY AN INCONVENIENT TRUTH BASED ON HIS BEST SELLING BOOK OF THE SAME NAME.

THIS IS REALLY NOT A POLITICAL ISSUE SO MUCH AS A MORAL ISSUE.

FUTURE GENERATIONS MAY WELL HAVE OCCASION TO ASK THEMSELVES, "WHAT WERE OUR PARENTS THINKING? WHY DIDN'T THEY WAKE UP WHEN THEY HAD A CHANCE?"

IT WEAVED FACTS, STORIES AND SPECULATION IN SUPPORT OF GORE'S BELIEF, THAT THE PLANET IS ON THE BRINK OF A SEVERE CLIMATE CRISIS.

AND THE FILM MADE AN IMPACT.

IT BROUGHT A NEW IMMEDIACY TO THE DEBATE OVER THE ENVIRONMENT.

IT EVEN WON AN OSCAR FOR BEST DOCUMENTARY IN 2007 AND A GRAMMY FOR BEST SPOKEN WORD ALBUM

AGAIN GORE BECAME A LIGHTNING ROD FOR BOTH PRAISE AND CRITICISM.

SOME SUGGEST HE DISTORTS THE SCIENCE, EXAGGERATES THE RISKS, AND ARGUES THOSE WHO CHALLENGE HIS ASSERTIONS ARE CORRUPT OR BLIND TO THE FACTS.

OTHERS POINT OUT INCONSISTENCIES WITH HIS OWN LIFESTYLE, SPECIFICALLY HIS OWN HOME.

BUT GORE'S HIGH PROFILE HAS ALWAYS MADE HIM A TARGET.

YET HE CONTINUES TO FOLLOW HIS TRUE CALLING;

I CHALLENGE OUR NATION TO COMMIT TO PRODUCING 100% OF OUR ELECTRICITY FROM RENEWABLE ENERGY WITHIN 10 YEARS

WECANSOLVEIT.ORG

IN 2007, 25 YEARS OF ADVOCACY FOR ENVIRONMENTAL ISSUES WERE REWARDED WHEN HE (WITH THE UN INTERGOVERNMENTAL PANEL ON CLIMATE CHANGE) WERE AWARDED THE NOBEL PEACE PRIZE.

WE HAVE THE ABILITY TO SOLVE THIS CRISIS AND AVOID THE WORST - THOUGH NOT ALL - OF ITS CONSEQUENCES, IF WE ACT BOLDLY, DECISIVELY AND QUICKLY.

CRITICIZE ME FOR NOT COVERING YOUR PET POLICY, YOUR FAVORITE GAFFE, OR YOUR PARTISAN AGENDA.

BUT MY JOB IN 22 PAGES WAS TO GIVE YOU A SENSE OF WHO AL GORE IS.

TO SOME HE IS AN ARROGANT, SCRIPTED LIBERAL HYPOCRITE...THE EMBODIMENT OF BIG INVASIVE GOVERNMENT.

OTHERS SEE HIM AS THE IDEALISTIC CONSCIENCE OF THE COUNTRY.

HE CAPTURES THIS DIVIDE IN HIS 2007 BOOK AN ASSAULT ON REASON.

AMERICAN DEMOCRACY IS NOW IN DANGER—NOT FROM ANY ONE SET OF IDEAS, BUT FROM UNPRECEDENTED CHANGES IN THE ENVIRONMENT WHICH IDEAS LIVE AND SPREAD.

BUT, NO MATTER WHAT SIDE OF THE POLITICAL FENCE YOU RESIDE, YOU MUST ADMIT THAT AL GORE IS ONE OF THE MORE IMPORTANT, ACCOMPLISHED, INFLUENTIAL AND RELEVANT POLITICIANS OF THE 21ST CENTURY.

★ POLITICAL ★ POWER ★

Al Gore

Scott Davis — **Writer**

Aldo Giordanelli Corbellini — **Penciler**

Simon Wright — **Colorist**

Wilson Ramos Jr. — **Letterer**

Darren G. Davis — **Graphics**

Cover: Patricio Carbajal

Patrick Foster
Logo Design

Adam Ellis
Production

Darren G. Davis
Publisher

Jason Schultz
Vice President

Lisa K. Brause
Entertainment Manager

Crystal VanDiver
Director

Lisa Battan
Marketing Director

Janda Tithia
Coordinator

Scott Davis
Media Manager

Kim Sherman
Marketing Director

Vonnie Harris
New Business

Adam Ellis
Coordinator

BLUEWATER COMICS

www.bluewaterprod.com

#ERASEHATE WITH THE MATTHEW SHEPARD FOUNDATION

With your donated dollars and volunteer hours, we work tirelessly to erase hate from every corner of America through our programs.

SPEAKING ENGAGEMENTS

Since Matt's death in 1998, Judy and Dennis have been determined to prevent others from similar tragedies. By sharing their story, they are able to carry on Matt's legacy.

HATE CRIMES REPORTING

Our work to improve reporting includes conducting trainings for law enforcement agencies, building relationships between community leaders and law enforcement, and developing policy reform in reporting practices.

LARAMIE PROJECT

MSF offers support to productions of The Laramie Project, which depicts the events leading up to and after Matt's murder. It remains one of the most performed plays in America.

MATTHEW'S PLACE

MatthewsPlace.com is a blog designed to provide young LGBTQ+ people with an outlet for their voices. From finance to health to love and dating, and everything in between, our writers contribute excellent material.

Erase Hate

Matthew
Shepard
Foundation
embracing diversity